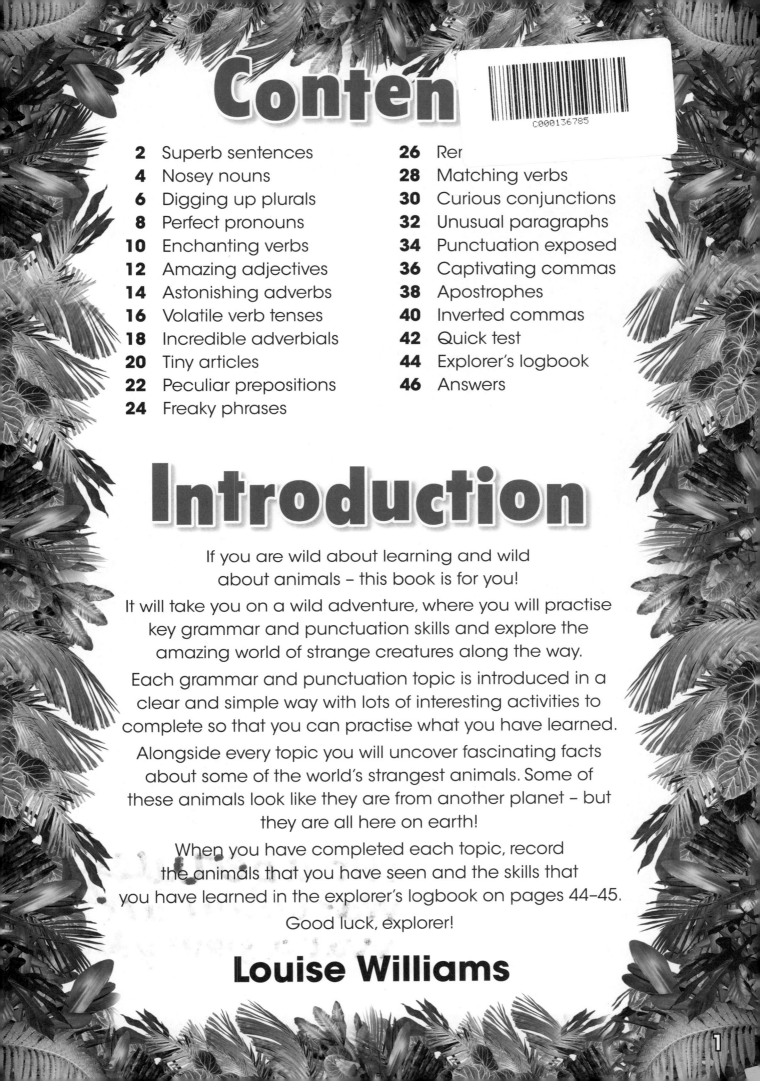

Conten

Introduction

If you are wild about learning and wild about animals – this book is for you!

It will take you on a wild adventure, where you will practise key grammar and punctuation skills and explore the amazing world of strange creatures along the way.

Each grammar and punctuation topic is introduced in a clear and simple way with lots of interesting activities to complete so that you can practise what you have learned.

Alongside every topic you will uncover fascinating facts about some of the world's strangest animals. Some of these animals look like they are from another planet – but they are all here on earth!

When you have completed each topic, record the animals that you have seen and the skills that you have learned in the explorer's logbook on pages 44–45.

Good luck, explorer!

Louise Williams

Superb sentences

A sentence is a set of words that make sense. A sentence starts with a capital letter.

It usually contains a **subject** and a **verb**.

Look at this example:

The bird danced

subject verb

FACT FILE

Animal:	Superb bird-of-paradise
Habitat:	Rainforests of New Guinea
Weight:	50 to 100 g
Lifespan:	Unknown
Diet:	Fruit, berries, seeds and insects

There are four types of sentence:

Type	Definition	End punctuation
Statement	gives **information**	full stop (.)
Question	needs an **answer**	question mark (?)
Exclamation	shows strong **emotion**	exclamation mark (!)
Command	**tells** someone to do something	full stop (.) or exclamation mark (!)

Task 1 The words in these sentences have been muddled. Rewrite them, putting the words in the correct order.

a It a bird beautiful is .

isir a beauesful brd-

b feathers are colour its What ?

Wat colour artios

c funny What a dance !

wat a sunny dace!

d photograph Take a . _____

Task 2

Each egg has a letter on it: S (statement), Q (question), E (exclamation) or C (command). Draw a line to join the sentence to its type.

a Look at that bird.

b What is it doing?

c Wow!

d It is hopping in circles.

(S)

(E)

(C)

(Q)

WILD FACT

The superb bird-of-paradise clears a 'dance floor', calls to the ladies, fans his feathers out and hops frantically whilst snapping his tail on the ground. Now if that doesn't impress them, I don't know what will!

Task 3

If you could ask the superb bird-of-paradise any question, what would it be?

Write your question on the line below.

_____

Exploring Further ...

Put the words in the feathers in the right order so that the sentence makes sense. Write the correct sentence on the line below. Remember to start with a **capital letter** and use the correct **punctuation** at the end of the sentence.

WILD FACT

Opposites attract. The female is mainly brown with a stripy head and breast, whilst the male has jet black feathers and a beautiful, shiny blue-green breast.

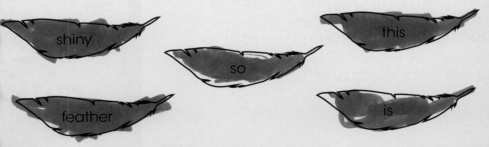

shiny

so

this

feather

is

rnis seacher is so shiny

Now flutter to pages 44–45 to record what you have learned in your explorer's logbook.

Nosey nouns

A **noun** is a naming word for a person, place, animal or thing.

Common nouns name a general kind of person, place, animal or thing:

boy   jungle   monkey   nose

Proper nouns name a particular person, place, day or month. These nouns always begin with a capital letter:

George   Paris   Tuesday   April

Collective nouns name a group of people, animals or things:

a <u>flock</u> of sheep

Task 1

Underline all the common nouns in these sentences.

a The monkey swung from the tree.

b Its nose is big and its tummy is too!

c They live near rivers and swamps.

d Can you hear the wind blowing?

e Proboscis monkeys only eat unripe fruit.

f Monkeys travel long distances to find food.

FACT FILE

Animal:	Proboscis monkey
Habitat:	Forests of Borneo
Weight:	20 kg
Lifespan:	20 years in captivity
Diet:	Leaves, seeds and unripe fruit

WILD FACT

When it is in danger, blood rushes to the proboscis monkey's nose. As it swells, it lets out a rather loud honking sound.

Task 2 Choose a collective noun from the box to complete each phrase.

crowd	troop	herd	bunch

a A _____ of flowers.

b A _____ of monkeys.

c A _____ of people.

d A _____ of cattle.

WILD FACT

What a splash! Proboscis monkeys love to swim. As they swing from tree to tree, sometimes they do a giant belly flop into the water.

Task 3 Rewrite these sentences including all the missing capital letters for the proper nouns.

a mr holt flew to asia in july to see the monkeys.

_____

b tom and betsy went to the jungle in borneo.

_____

c saturday is when uncle ben comes to visit.

_____

d borneo is an island in south east asia.

_____

Exploring Further ...

Find five common nouns using the letters from the monkey's name.

PROBOSCIS MONKEY

a You use this to unlock a door.   _____

b You wear it on your foot.   _____

c The son of a king is called this.   _____

d If you are rich, you have a lot of this. _____

e This shines in the sky at night.   _____

Now swing to pages 44–45 to record what you have learned in your explorer's logbook.

5

Digging up plurals

Nouns can be **singular** or **plural**.

Singular means one:

mole   hole

Plural means **more than one**:

moles   holes

A **regular plural noun** is formed by adding **s** or **es** to the end of a word.

mammal ⟶ *mammals*

fox ⟶ *foxes*

An **irregular plural** is formed in different ways.

foot ⟶ *feet*

mouse ⟶ *mice*

FACT FILE

Animal: Star-nosed mole
Habitat: Wetlands of eastern North America
Weight: 55 g
Lifespan: 3 to 4 years
Diet: Aquatic worms and insects

WILD FACT

The star-nosed mole has the best sense of touch of any mammal in the world. It is the only animal that can smell under water and is the fastest eater, too.

Task 1   **Underline all the plural nouns in the sentences below.**

a   Those moles are excellent diggers.

b   They blow bubbles under water.

c   Their noses help them to sense worms and beetles.

d   Children love these crazy creatures.

e   Moles have round bodies, large claws and fleshy snouts.

Task 2 Change the singular noun in brackets into an irregular plural noun. Write it on the line.

a The star-nosed mole has 44 ＿＿＿＿＿ (**tooth**).

b It has large, scaly ＿＿＿＿＿ (**foot**).

c Most ＿＿＿＿＿ (**person**) have good eyesight, unlike moles.

d Moles like to swim but ＿＿＿＿＿ (**sheep**) do not.

e The moles spend most of their ＿＿＿＿＿ (**life**) in water.

Task 3 Write the plural form of these nouns.

a calf ＿＿＿＿＿＿＿   b wolf ＿＿＿＿＿＿＿

c wife ＿＿＿＿＿＿＿   d leaf ＿＿＿＿＿＿＿

e shelf ＿＿＿＿＿＿＿   f elf ＿＿＿＿＿＿＿

g thief ＿＿＿＿＿＿＿   h loaf ＿＿＿＿＿＿＿

WILD FACT

The star-nosed mole has large, scaly feet to help it dig quickly. Its favourite prize? A big juicy worm.

Exploring Further ...

Write the singular of these plural nouns and then find them in the word-search. The first has been done for you.

children: *child*

foxes: ＿＿＿＿＿＿＿

geese: ＿＿＿＿＿＿＿

ladies: ＿＿＿＿＿＿＿

deer: ＿＿＿＿＿＿＿

men: ＿＿＿＿＿＿＿

women: ＿＿＿＿＿＿＿

people: ＿＿＿＿＿＿＿

F	D	K	M	C	K	E
O	X	L	Y	G	P	S
X	B	D	I	E	W	O
M	A	U	R	H	E	O
L	A	S	D	N	C	G
H	O	N	A	M	O	W
N	I	D	E	E	R	S

Now dig your way to pages 44–45 to record what you have learned in your explorer's logbook.

7

Perfect pronouns

Pronouns are short words that **replace** nouns or **refer** to nouns. They are often used so that the noun is not repeated. This makes our writing more cohesive.

Here are the **personal pronouns**:

I   me   we   us   you   he   him   she   her   it   they   them

Look at this example:

Pippa looked for the octopus but <u>she</u> couldn't see <u>it</u>.

Here are the **possessive pronouns**:

my   mine   your   yours   his   her   hers   its   our   ours   their   theirs

Look at this example:

Ellie borrowed my goggles as <u>mine</u> were better than <u>hers</u>.

Task 1

Underline the personal pronouns in these sentences.

a <u>It</u> has eight <u>arms</u>.

b Don't <u>they</u> look like Dumbo!

c Can <u>you</u> see that octopus?

d <u>I</u> think it saw us.

e Sharks and killer whales like to eat <u>them</u>.

f <u>You</u> can't dive as deep as the dumbo octopus!

Task 2

Choose a suitable **possessive pronoun** and write it on the line to complete these sentences.

a The octopus flapped __its__ ear-like fins.

b Sonny and Pearl loved __shur__ trip to the zoo.

c "Come and see __the__ shells!" we cried.

d __the__ camera is just like __his__ .

WILD FACT

You are unlikely to bump into this unique creature. The dumbo octopus is extremely rare. It lives right at the bottom of the deepest, darkest waters.

Task 3

Tick one box to show the pair of pronouns that completes the sentence.

Cheryl watched a film about enchanting sea creatures and _____ loved _____.

he him ☐   she it ✓

they them ☐   we her ☐

Exploring Further ...

Memory game: read each of the pronouns in the octopus THREE times.

me   yours
you   our
she   it
he   him   your
their
they   her
his   hers

Now cover the picture and write down as many of the pronouns as you can remember.

_____

_____

Now float to pages 44–45 to record what you have learned in your explorer's logbook.

Enchanting verbs

FACT FILE

Animal: Leafy sea dragon
Habitat: Coastal waters of southern Australia
Weight: 110 g
Lifespan: 5 to 10 years
Diet: Shrimp, crustaceans and plankton

Every sentence must contain a **verb**. A verb is a **doing** or a **being** word.

Here are some examples of **doing** words:

run   shout   splash   dive   jump

Here are some examples of **being** words:

am   are   is   was   were   will be

Task 1   Circle all the verbs around the leafy sea dragon.

swim

suck

glide

dragon

leaf

breathe

float

orange

seahorse

blow

Task 2   Underline the verbs in each sentence.

a   The sea dragon <u>sways</u> like seaweed.

b   Bony plates cover its body. ?

c   <u>They</u> suck food into their tube-like snouts.

d   These creatures are very rare.

e   Leafy sea dragons glide and tumble through the water.

f   You will be lucky if you see one.

WILD FACT

These mysterious fish can change colour, rotate their eyes independently and fool predators into thinking they are just a piece of seaweed!

Task 3   Choose a suitable verb to complete each sentence.

a   Female sea dragons _____ 250 eggs.

b   They _____ in rocky reefs and seaweed beds.

c   Sea dragons _____ gracefully through the ocean.

d   Their eggs _____ in eight weeks.

e   The sea dragons _____ well camouflaged.

WILD FACT

The female leafy sea dragon lays up to 250 bright pink eggs. The male carries the eggs on his tail for 8 weeks until they hatch. Only about 10 eggs survive.

Exploring Further ...

Find the verbs hidden in this 'verb wave' to describe how a sea dragon moves. Write them on the lines below.

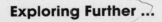

swaysglidesfloatsdriftsswimsdivessailsskims

_____

_____

Now drift to pages 44–45 to record what you have learned in your explorer's logbook.

Amazing adjectives

Adjectives are **describing** words. They tell us more about a noun or pronoun.

In these examples, the adjectives are underlined:

the <u>deep</u> sea   the <u>large</u> crab

Comparative adjectives compare two nouns, like this:

The crab is <u>bigger</u> than the spider.

The crab is <u>more colourful</u> than the spider.

The spider is <u>less interesting</u> than the crab.

Superlative adjectives compare more than two nouns, like this:

The coconut crab is the <u>biggest</u> land crab.

The coconut crab is the <u>most colourful</u> crab.

The brown crab is the <u>least interesting</u> crab.

Task 1   Look at the words below. Circle the adjectives.

a rough sea

b hungry crab

c bright blue sky

d awesome claws

e powerful pincers

f island home

Task 2

Underline all the adjectives in this passage.

The huge crab with its strong legs and sharp claws climbed the coconut tree. It cracked open the hard shell and ate the soft flesh. Then it ate juicy fruits and tasty nuts. It was a delicious meal and the crab was very happy.

How many did you find? _____

WILD FACT

The coconut crab can climb trees! Its powerful claws are strong enough to lift most eight-year-old children … but luckily they prefer coconuts!

Task 3

Write the correct adjectives in the spaces in the table.

adjective	comparative	superlative
large	larger	largest
strong		
	funnier	
		most beautiful
		tastiest
high		
	more careful	

Exploring Further …

Look at this beach scene. Can you find some interesting adjectives to describe the objects in the picture?

_____

_____

_____

_____

Now crawl to pages 44–45 to record what you have learned in your explorer's logbook.

13

Astonishing adverbs

Adverbs tell us more about a verb. They often tell us **how**, **when** or **where** something happens or how it is done.

Many adverbs end with the suffix **ly**.

The lizard burrowed eagerly.

verb   adverb (how)

Task 1   Circle the adverbs in these sentences.

a The fox quickly dropped the lizard.

b Frantically, the lizard dug a hole in the sand.

c The lizard fearfully shot blood from its eyes.

d The fox's head shook violently.

e He was very surprised.

f This lizard narrowly escaped!

g The fox ran off hungrily.

h He was seldom defeated.

Task 2

Choose suitable adverbs to fill the gaps and write them on the lines.

a The fox growled _____ and _____ at the tiny lizard.

b The lizard sunbathed _____ and _____ in the hot sun.

c The sun shone _____ and _____ over the desert.

d The lizard flicked his tongue out _____ and _____ at the ant.

e The snake lifted his head _____ and saw the lizard moving _____.

WILD FACT

Short-horned lizards have a crown of 'horns' on the back of their head. They can inflate their bodies up to twice their size when under attack – like a spiky balloon!

Task 3

Choose an adverb from the box to complete the sentences. Use one word for each sentence.

yesterday	rarely	never	usually

a The lizard _____ eats ants and beetles.

b It was scorching hot _____.

c I hope it _____ shoots blood at me!

d Ants will _____ escape its fast tongue.

WILD FACT

When spiny skin is not enough, the short-horned lizard scares predators with a truly astonishing tactic: it squirts blood from its eyes!

Exploring Further ...

Search each row of this word maze to find 5 hidden adverbs.

A	H	D	Q	U	I	C	K	L	Y	S	O
P	E	L	A	N	G	R	I	L	L	Y	O	K
E	S	L	O	W	L	Y	W	L	O	F	E
F	B	P	N	L	O	U	D	L	Y	D	Y
U	L	A	Z	I	L	Y	D	O	D	B	Z

Now scuttle to pages 44–45 to record what you have learned in your explorer's logbook.

15

Volatile verb tenses

Verbs can change the tense of a sentence. The **tense** of a verb tells us **when** an action takes place.

Past ———→ Present ———→ Future

The **past** tense has **already happened**:

The shrimp <u>moved</u> quickly.

The **present** tense is **happening now**.

The shrimp <u>moves</u> / <u>is moving</u> quickly.

The **future** tense **will happen**.

The shrimp <u>will move</u> quickly.

The **present perfect** tense **connects** the present to the past.

The shrimp <u>has moved</u> quickly.

Task 1 Change these verbs into the past tense. Choose one word for each.

saw	flew	thought	boiled	swam	threw

a swim _____

b think _____

c fly _____

d see _____

e throw _____

f boil _____

Task 2   Draw a line to show the tense of each of these sentences.

a   The mantis shrimp is hiding.

b   Will that crab escape the mantis shrimp?

c   It moved too fast.

d   The crab has died.

e   The mantis shrimp punches its prey.

past

present perfect

present

present

future

Task 3   Circle the correct form of the present perfect tense verbs in these sentences.

a   I have <u>see / seen</u> it before.

b   They have <u>catched / caught</u> a shrimp.

c   Its aggressive punch has <u>wounded / wound</u> the crab.

d   The female has <u>lain / laid</u> two clutches of eggs.

e   The mantis shrimp <u>have / has</u> struck its prey.

WILD FACT

With bulging eyes and sharp claws, the mantis shrimp strikes its prey at the speed of a bullet. In fact, it moves so fast that the water actually boils!

Exploring Further ...

Change this passage from the present tense into the past tense. Write the past tense of each underlined verb in the box above it.

It <u>hides</u> in the sand and <u>waits</u> patiently. A tasty crab <u>crawls</u> by. The

mantis shrimp <u>rolls</u> its bulging eyes then <u>pounces</u> like lightening. It <u>stabs</u> its

prey and <u>begins</u> to feast.

Now shoot to pages 44–45 to record what you have learned in your explorer's logbook.

17

Incredible adverbials

An **adverbial phrase** is a group of words that **acts like an adverb**.

It gives us more information about **how, when or where** something is done.

The frog hopped <u>as quick as a flash</u>. (tells us **how**)

Fronted adverbials are adverbs or adverbial phrases placed at the **beginning** of a sentence. They are followed by a comma.

<u>After nightfall</u>, the frog feeds. (tells us **when**)

Sometimes an adverbial phrase is also a **prepositional phrase**.

The frog hopped <u>on to the leaf</u>. (tells us **where**)

FACT FILE

Animal: Glass frog
Habitat: Rainforests of Central and South America
Weight: Less than 28 g
Lifespan: 10 to 14 years
Diet: Insects and spiders

WILD FACT

No need to X-ray a glass frog. This incredible amphibian has transparent skin, meaning you can see right through it! You can even see its tiny heart pumping.

Task 1 Underline the adverbial phrase in each sentence.

a Glass frogs lay eggs on top of leaves.

b They mate during wet weather.

c When resting on a leaf, they are hard to see.

d After two weeks, the tadpoles emerge.

e With bulging eyes, glass frogs see in all directions.

Task 2 The adverbial phrase in bold text tells us **how, when** or **where** something happens. Decide which we are being told in each sentence. Write **how, when** or **where** on the line.

a **At night**, the frog hunts for prey.   _____

b The glass frog lives **in the trees**.   _____

c They leap at prey **with open mouths**.   _____

d They hide from predators **by keeping very still**.   _____

e They mate **in the rainy season**.   _____

f Females lay eggs **on the undersides of leaves**.   _____

Task 3 Write a different fronted adverbial at the start of each sentence.

a _____, the frog ate the spider.

b _____, the snake spotted the frog.

c _____, it began to rain heavily.

d _____, the frog laid her eggs.

WILD FACT

The glass frog would definitely win a game of hide and seek. It is only about the size of a fingernail and its translucent lime-green skin is excellent camouflage.

Exploring Further ...

Rearrange the phrases to create a sentence. Try to begin with a fronted adverbial.

| cautiously |
| just then |
| over the edge | of the glossy leaf |
| the glass frog | peeped |

_____

_____

Now hop to pages 44–45 to record what you have learned in your explorer's logbook.

Tiny articles

A **determiner** stands before a noun or noun phrase.

An **article** is a tiny word that is a type of determiner.

There are three articles: **the**, **a**, and **an**.

The **definite article** is **the**. We use it to refer to something specific.

The jerboa over there.

The **indefinite article** is **a** or **an**. We use it to refer to something general.

We use **a** before a word beginning with a consonant or a consonant sound:

a jerboa   a unicorn (unicorn begins with a 'y' sound)

We use **an** before a word beginning with a vowel or a silent h.

an egg   an honour

Task 1   Decide whether to write **a** or **an** before each of these words.

a _____ mammal   **b** _____ insect   **c** _____ hour

d _____ hamster   **e** _____ useful skill   **f** _____ dark night

g _____ ear   **h** _____ group   **i** _____ area

FACT FILE

Animal:	Long-eared jerboa
Habitat:	Deserts of China and Mongolia
Weight:	24 to 38 g
Lifespan:	2 to 3 years
Diet:	Insects and plants

Task 2 Which sentences use correct articles? Put a ✓ or a ✗ in the box.

a An jerboa has enormous ears. ☐

b Its main predator is a owl. ☐

c They live in the desert. ☐

d It eats the insect every day. ☐

e An owl flies silently towards the jerboa. ☐

WILD FACT

The long-eared jerboa is a tiny mouse-sized rodent that hops around the desert like a kangaroo. Its ears are enormous compared with the rest of its body.

Task 3 Choose **a**, **an** or **the** to fill in the gaps in these sentences.

a Jerboas hunt during _____ night when _____ desert is cooler.

b The jerboa has _____ very long tail and _____ excellent sense of smell.

c If it hears _____ owl or _____ fox, _____ jerboa must hide.

d The desert is _____ very hard place to live in.

e _____ jerboa leaps in _____ zigzag way to avoid predators.

WILD FACT

Jerboas are nocturnal, meaning they are active at night. Their impressive ears mean that although they cannot see, they can hear almost everything – even a sleeping insect!

Exploring Further ...

Can you think of eight animals that live in the desert?

Write them on the lines in the sand using either **a** or **an** before each animal.

_____   _____

_____   _____

_____   _____

_____   _____

Now spring to pages 44–45 to record what you have learned in your explorer's logbook.

Peculiar prepositions

FACT FILE

Animal: Pink fairy armadillo

Habitat: Sandy plains and dry grasslands in Argentina

Weight: 120g

Lifespan: 5 to 10 years

Diet: Ants, worms and plant material

Prepositions show the relationship of one thing to another. They link nouns or pronouns to other words in a sentence.

Some common prepositions are:

in   on   under   above   through   after   before

Prepositions can show position according to **place** or **time**.

The armadillo was <u>on</u> the sand. (place)

The armadillo dug <u>during</u> the night. (time)

Task 1   Colour in all the bugs that contain a preposition.

below   pink   inside   over   sand

Task 2 — Underline the prepositions in each sentence.

a The armadillo burrowed under the ant hill.

b It used its large claws to move through the sand.

c Armadillos spend a lot of time below the ground.

d Their fur keeps them warm during cold nights.

e Above the ground, they risk being eaten.

f A thin membrane runs along its spine.

WILD FACT

Pink fairy armadillos are excellent diggers. In fact, they can bury themselves in a matter of seconds if threatened.

Task 3 — Complete each sentence with a suitable preposition.

a It has a pink shell _____ its back.

b The ant hides _____ the rock.

c The dog leapt _____ the armadillo.

d The armadillo curled _____ a tight ball.

e It dug down _____ the surface of the sand.

WILD FACT

The pink fairy armadillo is the smallest species of armadillo and is the only one that has its shell completely separate from its body.

Exploring Further ...

Find these prepositions in the word-search grid.

above
along
over
under
after
through
beneath
below

T	D	I	L	G	A	O	T
H	L	V	A	B	O	V	E
R	T	P	F	L	U	E	R
O	O	A	T	A	O	R	D
U	N	D	E	R	U	N	S
G	F	A	R	N	R	M	G
H	S	L	J	C	E	I	B
U	B	W	O	L	E	B	S

Now burrow your way to pages 44–45 to record what you have learned in your explorer's logbook.

23

Freaky phrases

FACT FILE

Animal: Aye aye
Habitat: Forests of Madagascar
Weight: 2 to 3 kg
Lifespan: Up to 23 years in captivity
Diet: Leaves, insects, larvae, fruit and nuts

A **phrase** is a small group of words that form part of sentence. There are two main types of phrases.

Noun phrases have a noun as their main word:

finger   long middle finger

↑   ↑

noun   noun phrase

Prepositional phrases begin with a preposition and will include a noun or a pronoun:

on   on the tree

↑   ↑

preposition   prepositional phrase

WILD FACT

Aye ayes are primates and are related to chimpanzees, apes and humans. They are the only primates thought to use echolocation to find prey, just like bats.

Task 1 Underline the noun phrases in each sentence.

a This very strange creature is adorable.

b No way! Its freaky middle finger scares me.

c Well, how else can it find a fat juicy grub?

d How clever! It's like a sharp fork.

e The perfect tool for a tricky job!

Task 2 Draw a line to join the first part of each sentence with a suitable prepositional phrase.

a   The bright moon shone   inside the hole.

b   The light wind rustled   above the forest.

c   The aye aye made a hole   with its teeth.

d   It stuck its long finger   from the hole.

e   The aye aye pulled a fat grub   through the leaves.

Task 3 Complete these sentences by adding a different adjective and a new prepositional phrase to each. The first one has been completed for you.

a   The **clever** aye aye can dangle easily **from the branches**.

b   The _____ aye aye popped a tasty grub _____.

c   The _____ aye aye climbed into his nest _____.

d   The _____ aye aye went to sleep _____.

Exploring Further ...

Write a sentence containing a noun phrase and a prepositional phrase to show where this little aye aye is hiding.

_____

_____

Now creep to pages 44–45 to record what you have learned in your explorer's logbook.

Remarkable clauses

A **clause** is a group of words containing a **subject** and a **verb**.

A **main clause** expresses a complete idea. It makes sense on its own.

The colugo glided.

subject   verb

A **subordinate clause** needs a main clause to make sense. Together they make a **complex sentence**.

The colugo glided until it reached the tree.

main clause   subordinate clause

A subordinate clause can come **before**, **after** or **in between** a main clause.

FACT FILE

Animal: Colugo
Habitat: Tropical rainforests of Southeast Asia
Weight: 1 to 2kg
Lifespan: Up to 15 years in captivity
Diet: Leaves, shoots, flowers, sap and fruit

WILD FACT

When resting, colugos use their strong claws to hang upside down from branches. They are clumsy climbers and avoid the ground for fear of predators.

Task 1 Write an **M** in the box if it is a main clause and write an **S** if it is a subordinate clause.

a the colugo gently glides ☐

b although it has no wings ☐

c it is a remarkable animal ☐

d when it is disturbed ☐

e the colugo has a huge membrane ☐

f unless it sees a predator ☐

Task 2 Underline the subordinate clause in each sentence.

a The colugo hung upside down because it needed a rest.

b It floated like a parachute until it reached the tree.

c The baby, which clung tightly to its mother, loved the flight!

d If I go to the rainforest, I hope to see a colugo.

e Unless we save the rainforest, the colugo will die out.

Task 3 Complete these sentences about the colugo by adding a main clause.

a When it saw the snake, _____.

b _____ because it was hungry.

c As the sun went down, _____.

d Although it was afraid, _____.

e _____, since the baby was so young.

WILD FACT

Is it a bird? Is it a plane? No – it's a colugo! This remarkable tree dweller stretches out a big piece of skin that connects its limbs and it glides like a kite for up to 100 metres!

Exploring Further …

Write a complex sentence to describe this picture.

_____

_____

Now glide to pages 44–45 to record have learned in your explorer's logbook.

Matching verbs

Most sentences have a **subject** and a **verb** which need to **match**. The subject is **who** or **what** the sentence is about. It must **agree** with the verb (the doing or being word).

Okapis are fascinating. ✓
Okapis is fascinating. ✗

They live in rainforests. ✓
They lives in rainforests. ✗

FACT FILE

Animal:	Okapi
Habitat:	Tropical forests of central Africa
Weight:	200 to 300 kg
Lifespan:	20 to 30 years
Diet:	Leaves, shoots, fruit and fungi

WILD FACT

The okapi's flexible, blue, 30-cm tongue is long enough to clean its eyes and ears. Just imagine being able to lick your own ears!

Task 1 Tick the box if the subject agrees with the verb in these sentences.

a Okapis eat many different plants. ☐

b That okapi have an amazing tongue. ☐

c It were in the rainforest. ☐

d The leopard is a predator. ☐

e The scientist done some research. ☐

Task 2 Circle the correct form of the verb.

a The okapis have / has stripes like a zebra.

b It is / are related to the giraffe.

c The hungry leopards stalks / stalk their prey.

d The baby drunk / drank its mother's milk.

e Okapis have / has a secretive nature.

WILD FACT

The beautiful okapi looks like a cross between a zebra, a horse and a giraffe! Its striped bottom is great camouflage when hiding in the forest.

Task 3 Rewrite these sentences, making sure the verbs are the correct tense and agree with their subjects.

a The little okapi were lost and hided in the forest until his mother finded him.

_____

b At birth, a baby okapi are 80 cm tall and weigh 16 kg!

_____

c The okapi's large, upright ears catches the smallest sounds.

_____

Exploring Further ...

Complete this verb crossword, using the correct verb forms.

Across

2. Okapis _____ my favourite animal

4. The okapi _____ in Africa.

5. A leopard can _____ an okapi by biting its throat.

Down

1. It _____ a very long tongue.

3. Okapis _____ plants.

4. They can _____ their ears!

Now dash to pages 44–45 to record what you have learned in your explorer's logbook.

Curious conjunctions

Conjunctions are **connecting** words. They **link** words, phrases or clauses.

Coordinating conjunctions join words, phrases or two main clauses:

for   and   nor   but   or   yet   so

The shoebill listens <u>and</u> waits.

Subordinating conjunctions join a subordinate clause to a main clause:

although   because   after   if   when   before

<u>When</u> it saw a fish, the shoebill lurched.

WILD FACT

The shoebill carries large gulps of water to cool down its chicks in the nest. The chicks make a 'hiccupping' sound as they beg for food.

Task 1   Circle the coordinating conjunctions in these sentences.

a The shoebill eats fish but it may eat baby crocodiles.

b Have you seen or heard the shoebill?

c Its bill is powerful and extremely sharp.

d They look like statues, yet they can move very fast.

e Their habitat is being destroyed, so the shoebill is at risk.

FACT FILE

Animal:	Shoebill
Habitat:	Freshwater swamps and dense marshes in East Africa
Weight:	4 to 7 kg
Lifespan:	Up to 35 years
Diet:	Fish, frogs, water snakes, lizards, turtles and young crocodiles

Task 2   Choose a subordinating conjunction from the box to complete the sentences below.

until   because   when   although

a The shoebill looks very curious _____ its beak is like a shoe.

b _____ it eats frogs and birds, it prefers lungfish.

c The bird waits patiently _____ it spots its prey.

d It moves as fast as lightning _____ it plunges at a fish.

WILD FACT

This curious prehistoric-looking bird has the most unusual beak, rather like a shoe! The razor-sharp hook at the end of its beak is sharp enough to slice the head off a very large fish.

Task 3   Join the two sentences in each line using different and suitable conjunctions. Write your sentence on the line below.

a I saw a shoebill falling over. It made me laugh.

_____

b I love musical statues. We played it at my party.

_____

Exploring Further ...

Help the shoebill get back to the egg.

Now circle the conjunction in this sentence:

The curious shoebill walked through the maze because he wanted to find his egg.

Now fly to pages 44–45 to record what you have learned in your explorer's logbook.

Unusual paragraphs

Paragraphs help to **organise** information. They contain one or more sentences. A new paragraph starts on a new line.

In **fiction**, paragraphs can show a change in time or place.

They are also used to introduce:

- new sections of a story
- new characters
- new speakers
- new themes

In **non-fiction**, paragraphs help to organise ideas and facts.

They sometimes start with subheadings and are used to:

- introduce new information
- introduce new points of view

Task 1   Write **T** beside the true statements and **F** beside the false statements.

a   Paragraphs help to organise information. ☐

b   A paragraph must have at least five sentences. ☐

c   A new paragraph starts on a new line. ☐

d   Paragraphs always have subheadings. ☐

e   Paragraphs occur in fiction and non-fiction. ☐

Task 2

Complete the sentence below using words in the tapir and commas where necessary.

new themes

new sections
or
new characters

new speakers   introduce

In fiction, paragraphs are used to _____

_____

_____

WILD FACT

The shy tapir looks like a mixture of a hippo and an overgrown pig. Its nose and lip join to make a snout which comes in useful as a snorkel for underwater dips.

Task 3

Read this extract and then colour in the leaf that contains the most suitable subheading.

All tapirs are herbivores and spend most of their time foraging for food. They eat leaves, twigs, branches, buds, shoots, berries and aquatic plants.

habitat   diet   size   species

WILD FACT

Tapirs communicate with a high-pitched whistle, which sounds like a car screeching to a halt! Snorting and foot-stamping mean they are ready for a fight.

Exploring Further ...

Read the story below. Put two slashes (like this //) where you think a new paragraph should begin.

One day, the baby tapir went for a wander in the forest. He wanted to find some tasty fruit. While he was roaming, he began to feel afraid. What if he met with danger? Suddenly, a loud roar erupted from the bushes. A terrifying tiger loomed. With a faint cry, the little tapir turned and ran until he found the comfort of his mother.

Now roam to pages 44–45 to record what you have learned in your explorer's logbook.

33

Punctuation exposed

Punctuation is used to help writing make sense. All sentences begin with a **capital letter** and most end with a **full stop**. Some sentences end with a **question mark** (?) to show that a question is being asked. Some sentences end with an **exclamation mark** (!) to show a strong emotion. These sentences are usually spoken in a louder voice.

WILD FACT

Foul food! Naked mole rats eat their own droppings. This helps the roots they eat to go down smoothly.

Task 1   Punctuate these sentences with either a full stop or a question mark.

a Where do naked mole rats live

b Why is their skin so wrinkly

c They can move their teeth like chopsticks

d Can you believe they can't feel pain

e Only the queen gives birth to young

Rewrite these sentences, using the correct punctuation.

a   can a naked mole rat run backwards

_____

b   they can run as fast backwards as forwards

_____

c   that's amazing Shall I try (hint: two sentences)

_____

d   don't be daft

_____

e   you will fall over

_____

Task 3   Draw a line to join each exclamation with a matching emotion.

a   Wow!   pain

b   Ouch!   panic

c   How dare you!   surprise

d   At last!   relief

e   I'm falling!   anger

WILD FACT

Naked mole rats live in huge groups of up to 300. Only the queen mole rat will produce babies. She bullies the other females to make sure that they do not reproduce.

Exploring Further ...

Write a sentence about this little naked mole rat making sure you use the correct punctuation.

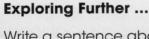

_____

_____

Now tunnel to pages 44–45 to record what you have learned in your explorer's logbook.

Captivating commas

Commas are punctuation marks that show when you need to take a brief pause. They are used in three main ways.

- To separate items in a list:

It eats <u>ants</u>, <u>termites</u>, <u>flies</u> and worms.

We do not use a comma before the **and**.

- To mark a fronted adverbial:

<u>Earlier that day</u>, the pangolin ate ants.

<u>Later on</u>, it ate some juicy flies.

- To separate extra information:

The ant, <u>which tried to escape</u>, was eaten.

WILD FACT

Pangolins do not have teeth, so they swallow small stones, which help to grind their food.

Task 1 Which one of these sentences uses commas correctly? Add a ✓ in the box.

a It has sharp, scales, long, claws, short, legs and a sticky tongue. ☐

b It has sharp scales, long claws, short legs, and a sticky tongue. ☐

c It has sharp scales, long claws, short legs and a sticky tongue. ☐

d It has, sharp scales, long claws, short legs and a sticky tongue. ☐

Task 2 Insert a comma after the fronted adverbial in the sentences below.

a Firstly the pangolin searched for ants.

b After a while he looked for some flies.

c Very carefully he dug for worms.

d Eventually he found some crickets.

e Happily he had plenty to eat.

Task 3 Use the information in the boxes to write a sentence. Add commas around the extra information and a full stop at the end.

| was riding on his mother's tail | which was very young | The baby pangolin |

_____

_____

Exploring Further ...

Complete this sentence using commas to separate the list of animals and the word 'and' before the final animal.

| fox   lemur   warthog   mongoose   meerkat   pangolin |

In the desert I saw a fox, _____

_____

_____

Now wobble to pages 44–45 to record what you have learned in your explorer's logbook.

37

Apostrophes

Apostrophes are punctuation marks that are used in two ways:

Apostrophes for **contraction** are used in informal writing to show that a letter or letters have been **missed out** when two words are joined.

do not ⟶ don't

it is ⟶ it's

I have ⟶ I've

Apostrophes for **possession** are used to show something or somebody belongs to a person or thing. If the owner is **singular**, add an apostrophe then **s**. Like this:

The seal's nose.

If the owner is **plural** and ends in an **s**, just add an apostrophe after the **s**, like this:

Those seals' noses.

Task 1 Complete these sentences by using an apostrophe to join the two words in brackets to make one contracted word.

a I (**can not**) _____ see the seals.

b (**They are**) _____ over there.

c (**It is**) _____ blowing a balloon!

d Quick! (**You will**) _____ miss it.

e I bet you (**could not**) _____ do that!

Task 2

Place the possessive apostrophe in the correct place.

a The seal pup was drinking her mothers milk.

b That seals hood is amazing!

c A polar bears temper knows no bounds.

d Hooded seals coats are grey with dark patches.

e The fishermans boat was stuck in the ice.

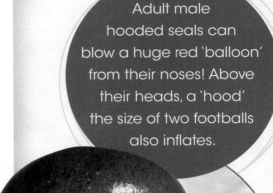

WILD FACT

Adult male hooded seals can blow a huge red 'balloon' from their noses! Above their heads, a 'hood' the size of two footballs also inflates.

Task 3

Rewrite these sentences using apostrophes where necessary.

a The polar bears meal couldnt be tastier!

_____

b The seals flipper was stuck in the fishermans net.

_____

c I cant see the sharks body, just its fin.

_____

Exploring Further ...

Rearrange the words so that the sentence makes sense. Write it on the line below.

| balloons baby blow can't they're because young too seals |

_____

Circle the two words that are contractions.

Now dive to pages 44–45 to record what you have learned in your explorer's logbook.

Inverted commas

Inverted commas (or speech marks) are used in **direct speech**. They show what a speaker actually says. The words that people say go **inside** the inverted commas:

"That red panda is adorable," said Mariam.

Direct speech starts with a capital letter (unless speech is interrupted):

Mariam said, *"That red panda is adorable."*

"That red panda," said Mariam, *"is adorable."* (interrupted)

FACT FILE

Animal:	Red panda
Habitat:	Mountainous forests of Nepal, north Burma and central China
Weight:	5.4 to 9 kg
Lifespan:	8 to 10 years
Diet:	Bamboo, fruit, insects and eggs

WILD FACT

Baby red pandas are usually born in holes inside trees. They look very cute and are covered in fluffy, grey hair.

Task 1 Put speech marks around what is being said in these sentences.

a Oh no! I cried.

b What's the matter? Dad asked.

c The leopard is watching the red panda, I replied.

d Well, Dad said hopefully, it may just be lucky.

e Make a noise to scare the leopard away, said Tom.

Task 2 Add full stops and commas to these sentences.

a "What's thats?" asked Karen

b "It looks like a racoon" Gregory giggled

c "No, I think it's a skunk" Yukiko smiled

d "Well, it's definitely not a cat" Charlie chirped

e "You're all wrong" said Jeremy "it's a red panda"

WILD FACT

Red pandas are stunning animals but, despite their name (and the fact that they love bamboo), they are not pandas at all! They are more like skunks or racoons.

Task 3 Which sentences are punctuated correctly? Put a ✓ or a ✗ in the box.

a "What a stunning animal, gasped Louise." ☐

b "It really is," agreed Charlotte. ☐

c "Look," Teresa said, it's curled up in a ball! ☐

d "Is it really a panda?" asked Ian. ☐

e I think so, said Thomas. ☐

f "I think they are really cute" smiled Ben. ☐

Exploring Further ...

Complete these sentences to show what the red panda may have said to the snow leopard.

Remember to use speech marks!

The frightened red panda cried, _____

The hungry snow leopard replied, _____

Now climb to pages 44–45 to record what you have learned in your explorer's logbook.

Quick test

Now try these questions. Give yourself 1 mark for every correct answer – but only if you answer each part of the question correctly.

1 **Is the following sentence a statement or a command?**

Look at that beautiful bird. _____

2 **Circle the four common nouns in this sentence.**

The monkey, which had a large nose, swung from the trees and landed in the water.

3 **Complete this sentence by changing the singular nouns in bold into plurals.**

The two little _____ (**mole**) were afraid of the two sly _____ (**fox**).

4 **Write a pronoun that could replace the underlined words.**

The octopus floated peacefully until <u>the octopus</u> saw a shark. _____

5 **Underline the verbs in this sentence.**

The sea dragon tumbled and drifted through the deep water.

6 **Change the bold word into a comparative adjective.**

Spiders are much _____ (**small**) than coconut crabs.

7 **Choose a suitable adverb from the box to complete this sentence.**

| happily   threateningly   gently |

The fierce fox growled _____ at the frightened lizard.

8 **Rewrite this sentence in the past tense.**

The mantis shrimp hides patiently and then flies at its prey.

_____

_____

9 **Underline the adverbial phrase in this sentence to show how the children stared.**

The children stared at the glass frog with great fascination.

10 **Complete this sentence with suitable articles.**

_____ tiny jerboa jumped high in _____ air when

it heard _____ terrifying sound.

42

11 **Circle the two prepositions in this sentence.**

The armadillo scuttled across the sand and into the burrow.

12 **Add a prepositional phrase (beginning with 'into') to expand this noun phrase.**

The curious aye aye poked his finger _____.

13 **The main clause is underlined in this sentence. True or false?**

As it needed a rest, <u>the colugo hung from the tree.</u> _____

14 **Tick the sentence with the correct verb form.**

The two little okapis was afraid of the leopard.

The two little okapis is afraid of the leopard.

The two little okapis were afraid of the leopard.

15 **Circle the conjunction in this sentence.**

The shoebill looks like a statue until it pounces at its prey.

16 **Paragraphs help to organise information and start on a new line. True or false?** _____

17 **Rewrite this sentence using the correct punctuation.**

do you know why the naked mole rat eats its own droppings

_____

18 **Insert a comma after the fronted adverbial.**

During the night the pangolin hunts for food.

19 **Circle the contraction which is spelt correctly.**

havent   haven't   have'nt   havn't

20 **Add speech marks to the dialogue below.**

Look at the red panda! Joss cried.

How did you do?   1–5 Try again!   6–10 Good try!   **/20**

11–15 Great work!   16–20 Excellent exploring!

Explorer's Logbook

Tick off the topics as you complete them and then colour in the star.

Superb sentences ☐

Perfect pronouns ☑

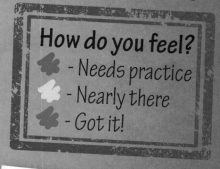

Astonishing adverbs ☐

Nosey nouns ☐

Enchanting verbs ☑

Volatile verb tenses ☐

Digging up plurals ☐

Amazing adjectives ☐

Incredible adverbials ☐

Tiny articles ☐

Matching verbs ☐

Captivating commas ☐

Peculiar prepositions ☐

Curious conjunctions ☐

Apostrophes ☐

Freaky phrases ☐

Unusual paragraphs ☐

Inverted commas ☐

Remarkable clauses ☐

Punctuation exposed ☐

Answers

Pages 2–3
Task 1
a It is a beautiful bird.
b What colour are its feathers?
c What a funny dance!
d Take a photograph.
Task 2
a C   **b** Q   **c** E   **d** S
Task 3
Answers will vary. All questions should begin with a capital letter and end with a question mark.
Exploring Further
This feather is so shiny.

Pages 4–5
Task 1
a monkey, tree   **b** nose, tummy
c rivers, swamps   **d** wind
e monkeys, fruit
f monkeys, distances, food
Task 2
a bunch   **b** troop   **c** crowd   **d** herd
Task 3
a Mr Holt flew to Asia in July to see the monkeys.
b Tom and Betsy went to the jungle in Borneo.
c Saturday is when Uncle Ben comes to visit.
d Borneo is an island in South East Asia.
Exploring Further
a key   **b** sock   **c** prince
d money   **e** moon

Pages 6–7
Task 1
a moles, diggers
b bubbles
c noses, worms, beetles
d children, creatures
e moles, bodies, claws, snouts
Task 2
a teeth   **b** feet   **c** people
d sheep   **e** lives
Task 3
a calves   **b** wolves   **c** wives
d leaves   **e** shelves   **f** elves
g thieves   **h** loaves
Exploring Further

F	D	K	M	C	K	E
O	X	L	Y	G	P	S
X	B	D	I	E	W	O
M	A	U	R	H	E	O
L	A	S	D	N	C	G
H	O	N	A	M	O	W
N	I	D	E	E	R	S

fox
goose
lady
deer
man
woman
person

Pages 8–9
Task 1
a It   **b** they   **c** you
d I, us   **e** them   **f** You

Task 2
Answers will vary. Accept any suitable possessive pronouns.
Task 3
she, it.

Pages 10–11
Task 1
Verbs: swim, breathe, glide, float, blow, suck
Task 2
a sways   **b** cover   **c** suck
d are   **e** glide, tumble   **f** will be, see
Task 3
Answers will vary.
Examples:
a lay   **b** live   **c** glide
d hatch   **e** are
Exploring Further
sways, glides, floats, drifts, swims, dives, sails, skims

Pages 12–13
Task 1
a rough   **b** hungry   **c** bright blue
d awesome   **e** powerful   **f** island
Task 2
huge, strong, sharp, coconut, hard, soft, juicy, tasty, delicious, happy (10)
Task 3
large, larger, largest
strong, stronger, strongest
funny, funnier, funniest
beautiful, more beautiful, most beautiful
tasty, tastier, tastiest
high, higher, highest,
careful, more careful, most careful
Exploring Further
Accept any suitable adjectives.

Pages 14–15
Task 1
a quickly   **b** frantically   **c** fearfully
d violently   **e** very   **f** narrowly
g hungrily   **h** seldom
Task 2
Answers will vary. Example answers:
a viciously, angrily
b happily, lazily
c brightly, fiercely
d quickly, hungrily
e slowly, cautiously
Task 3
a usually   **b** yesterday
c never   **d** rarely
Exploring Further

A	H	D	Q	U	I	C	K	L	Y	S
P	E	L	A	N	G	R	I	L	Y	O
E	S	L	O	W	L	Y	W	L	O	F
F	B	P	N	L	O	U	D	L	Y	D
U	L	A	Z	I	L	Y	D	O	D	B

46

Task 1

a	swam	**b**	thought	**c**	flew
d	saw	**e**	threw	**f**	boiled

Task 2

a	present	**b**	future	**c**	past
d	present perfect	**e**	present		

Task 3

a	seen	**b**	caught	**c**	wounded
d	laid	**e**	has		

Exploring Further

hid, waited, crawled, rolled, pounced, stabbed, began

Pages 18–19

Task 1

a on top of leaves
b during wet weather
c When resting on a leaf
d After two weeks
e With bulging eyes

Task 2

a	when	**b**	where	**c**	how
d	how	**e**	when	**f**	where

Task 3

Answers will vary.

Exploring Further

Sentences will vary. Example: Just then, the glass frog peeped cautiously over the edge of the glossy leaf.

Pages 20–21

Task 1

a	a	**b**	an	**c**	an
d	a	**e**	a	**f**	a
g	an	**h**	a	**i**	an

Task 2

Correct: **c, e**

Task 3

a	the, the	**b**	a, an	**c**	an, a, a (or the)
d	a	**e**	the (or a), a		

Exploring Further

Answers will vary. Accept any desert animal which correctly uses the indefinite article.

Pages 22–23

Task 1

Prepositions: below, inside, over

Task 2

a	under	**b**	through	**c**	of, below
d	during	**e**	above	**f**	along

Task 3

a on
b behind, under
c on to, at, towards, over
d into
e below

Exploring Further

T	D	I	L	G	A	O	T
H	L	V	A	B	O	V	E
R	T	P	F	L	U	E	R
O	O	A	T	A	O	R	D
U	N	D	E	R	U	N	S
G	F	A	R	N	R	M	G
H	S	L	J	C	E	I	B
U	B	W	O	L	E	B	S

Pages 24–25

Task 1

N.B. Also accept answers that do not include the modifiers.

a This very strange creature
b Its freaky middle finger
c a fat juicy grub
d a sharp fork
e the perfect tool, a tricky job

Task 2

a	above the forest.	**b**	through the leaves.
c	with its teeth.	**d**	inside the hole.
e	from the hole.		

Task 3

Accept any appropriate sentence.

Exploring Further

Accept any appropriate sentence.

Pages 26–27

Task 1

Main: **a, c, e**
Subordinate: **b, d, f**

Task 2

a because it needed a rest
b until it reached the tree
c which clung tightly to its mother
d If I go to the rainforest
e Unless we save the rainforest

Task 3

Answers will vary. Accept any with suitable main clause.

Exploring Further

Accept any appropriate complex sentence.
Example: Before it jumped, the colugo clutched the tree.

Pages 28–29

Task 1

Correct: **a, d**

Task 2

a	has	**b**	is	**c**	stalk
d	drank	**e**	have		

Task 3

a The little okapi <u>was</u> lost and <u>hid</u> in the forest until his mother <u>found</u> him.
b At birth, a baby okapi <u>is</u> 80 cm tall and <u>weighs</u> 16 kg!
c The okapi's large, upright ears <u>catch</u> the smallest sounds.

Exploring Further

Across: 2. are 4. lives 5. kill
Down: 1. has 3. eat 4. lick

Pages 30–31

Task 1

a	but	**b**	or	**c**	and
d	yet	**e**	so		

Task 2

a	because	**b**	although
c	until	**d**	when

Task 3

Answers will vary. Accept any suitable conjunction.
Examples:

a <u>When</u> I saw the Shoebill falling it over, it made me laugh.
b I love musical statues <u>so</u> we played it at my party.

Exploring Further

because

Pages 32–33

Task 1

a T   b F   c T   d F   e T

Task 2

Answer: …introduce new sections, new characters, new themes or new speakers. (Any order acceptable)

Task 3

Diet

Exploring Further

One day, the baby Tapir went for a wander in the forest. He wanted to find some tasty fruit.**//** While he was roaming, he began to feel afraid. What if he met with danger?**//** Suddenly, a loud roar erupted from the bushes. A terrifying tiger loomed.**//** With a faint cry, the little Tapir turned and ran until he found the comfort of his mother.

Pages 34–35

Task 1

a ?   b ?   c .   d ?   e .

Task 2

a   Can a naked mole rat run backwards?
b   They can run as fast backwards as forwards.
c   That's amazing! Shall I try?
d   Don't be daft!
e   You will fall over!

Task 3

a surprise   b pain   c anger
d relief   e panic

Exploring Further

Accept any correctly punctuated sentence.

Pages 36–37

Task 1

Correct: **c**

Task 2

a   Firstly, the pangolin searched for ants.
b   After a while, he looked for some flies.
c   Very carefully, he dug for worms.
d   Eventually, he found some crickets.
e   Happily, he had plenty to eat.

Task 3

The baby pangolin, which was very young, was riding on his mother's tail.

Exploring Further

In the desert I saw a fox, a lemur, a warthog, a mongoose, a meerkat and a pangolin.

Pages 38–39

Task 1

a can't   b They're   c It's
d You'll   e couldn't

Task 2

a mother's   b seal's   c bear's
d seals'   e fisherman's

Task 3

a   The polar bear's meal couldn't be tastier!
b   The seal's flipper was stuck in the fisherman's net.
c   I can't see the shark's body, just its fin.

Exploring Further

Baby seals <u>can't</u> blow balloons because <u>they're</u> too young.

Pages 40–41

Task 1

a   "Oh no!" I cried.
b   "What's the matter?" Dad asked.
c   "The leopard is watching the red panda," I replied.
d   "Well," Dad said hopefully, "it may just be lucky."
e   "Make a noise to scare the leopard away," said Tom.

Task 2

a   "What's that?" asked Karen.
b   "It looks like a racoon," Gregory giggled.
c   "No, I think it's a skunk," Yukiko smiled.
d   "Well, it's definitely not a cat," Charlie chirped.
e   "You're all wrong," said Jeremy, "it's a red panda."

Task 3

Correct: **b, d, f**

Exploring Further

Answers will vary but should be correctly punctuated.

Answers to quick test

1 command
2 monkey, nose, trees, water
3 moles, foxes
4 it
5 tumbled, drifted
6 smaller
7 threateningly
8 The mantis shrimp hid patiently then flew at its prey.
9 The children stared at the glass frog <u>with great fascination</u>.
10 a/the, the, a/the
11 across, into
12 into the hole / tree / the hole in the tree.
13 True
14 The two little okapis were afraid of the leopard.
15 until
16 True
17 Do you know why the naked mole rat eats its own droppings?
18 During the night, the pangolin hunts for food.
19 haven't
20 "Look at the red panda!" Joss cried.